Robin

HOW TO
DO SEX
PROPERLY

Thought it was about time
you learnt

love

Tuffy ⊗

APOLOGY

This book is not meant to give offence to anyone. In order not to be rude, where intimate details need to be illustrated we have used bear models. We apologise if this causes any distress to bears.

HOW TO
DO SEX
PROPERLY

by
"A Team of Experts"

or Bruce Aiken, Bridgid Herridge
and Colin Rowe

a Charles Herridge Book
published by
Frederick Muller Limited
London SW19 7JU

First published in Great Britain in 1982
by
Frederick Muller Limited
London SW19 7JU

Produced by Charles Herridge Limited
Tower House, Abbotsham, Devon
Designed and illustrated by
Bruce Aiken and Colin Rowe
Typeset by Lens Typesetting, Bideford, Devon
Printed in Italy by New Interlitho, SpA, Milan

ISBN 0 584 95020 9 (cased edition)
ISBN 0 584 95022 5 (limp edition)

CONTENTS

The Loud Report: The Sex Myth Exploded   6
How Will Sex Change Me?   8
Who to Do It With   10
Making the Most Of Yourself   12
Construct Your Ideal Partner   14
Are You Normal?   16
Learning to Kiss Right   18
Erogenous Zones   20
Fumble-Free Undressing   22
Postural Variations   24
Body Language   26
It Pays to Advertise   28
Digital Dating   30
Correspondence Course   32
What Went Wrong?   34
First Aid: Emergency Action   36
The Perils of Partytime: A Mating Game   38
Caught in the Act *or* Coitus Interruptus   40
Fetishes and Deviations   42
The Problem of Self-Abuse   44
The Facts of Life   46
Erotic Fantasies: Sex Without Tears   48
Sex: A Psychologist Explains   50
Sex and Your Stars   52
Your Questions Answered   54
Glossary   56
Index   58
So You Don't Like Sex   60
Your Diploma   62

THE LOUD REPORT

THE SEX MYTH EXPLODED

The recent publication of the long-awaited Loud Report* has exploded all the accepted myths and ideas about Sex.

PROBE

Ms Loud, who heads the International Ongoing Integrated Procedure and Structure Evaluation Project on Socio-sexual Performance, sent out detailed questionnaires to everyone in the world.

SEARCHING

The questions dealt with every sexually-related topic she could think of – from acne to zygotes. She asked pertinent and searching questions such as:

What is it?

What is it for?

Who should you do it with?

What should it look like?

How do you meet it?

What do you talk to it about?

Who goes where?

What do you do with your elbows?

Are you normal?

What is an erogenous zone?

Do yours work?

FLOODS

The answers came flooding back from people of all sexes, ages, occupations, races, creeds, social classes and union affiliations –

accountants, B movie actors, cannibals, dog-trainers, economists, Fascists, grandmothers, housewives, illusionists, Jeff Chandler look-alikes, kleptomaniacs, loss adjusters, Michael Parkinson, nuns, opticians, pygmies, queens, rapists, sexologists, teddy bears, underwear salesmen, vicars, window cleaners, xenophobes, yodellers, zoologists and many more, revealed their innermost secrets.

A BIG ONE

Supported by research grants from the Roosevelt Teddy Bear Institute and the Cosytoes Continental Quilt Company, Ms Loud has spent the last three weeks compiling the actual answers and the result is a 3 million page report which proves conclusively that which many of us had only suspected up to now,

> 99.9% OF PEOPLE
> DON'T KNOW
> HOW TO
> DO SEX
> PROPERLY

From the data she has received Ms Loud has extrapolated an amazing picture of your sex lives (see graph IA(i)).

As you can see, Sex is a lot more complicated than you thought, and most people have failed to master even its most basic aspects.

A SEMINAL REPORT

The frank replies of all those interrogated are reproduced in full in the report – not one word has been omitted. Strict anonymity was, of course, guaranteed. The answers show an almost total ignorance of the essential facts of life.

97% of systems analysts in Idaho don't even know what "It" is. Even the Editor of the Oxford English Dictionary (anon.) thinks it is "the sum of those differences in the structure and function of the reproduction organs on the grounds of which beings are distinguished as male and female, and of other physiological differences consequent on these". Now, with filth like that floating around in his or her mind he or she isn't go to get very far in life – is he or she?

Such misconceived ideas are typical of the sort of replies Ms Loud had to ponder over.

87% of the world expert sexologists got very excited about "pervicacious gonadal urges" when asked "what is 'It' for?", but the Vatican was even further from the mark.

The Loud Report on Socio-sexual Anatomic Structuring and Psychogenic Response and Stimulation Situations (or ROSSASPRASS) published by IPSEP Publications.

Graph IA (i) PHYSIO-PSYCHIC REACTION PATTERNS AMONG ACTIVE STUDY SUBJECT POPULATIONS

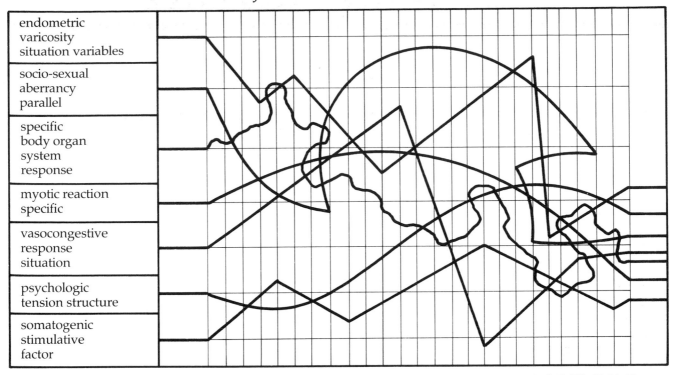

endometric varicosity situation variables																									
socio-sexual aberrancy parallel																									
specific body organ system response																									
myotic reaction specific																									
vasocongestive response situation																									
psychologic tension structure																									
somatogenic stimulative factor																									

A B C D K L M N O T U V P Q R S E F G H I J W X Y Z

Several people thought they knew *who* to do it with. Mr M.B. of The Marina, Antibes, wasn't far wrong. But as for what "It" should look like – nobody seems to know.

An amazing variety of extraordinary contortions were offered for "who goes where?", all of them totally impossible, and some of them (especially the one from Mr X of Apartment 92, 8 Wombat Road, Wagga Wagga, N.S.W., Australia) were downright rude!

The elbow problem is universal. 8000,000,000,000 people don't know what to do with them. Mr A., an optician from Amsterdam is typical. "They get in the way every time I attempt it, and I have suffered severe grazing on several occasions. I tried using padded bandages but then I couldn't bend my arms and got into an even worse mess."

And so the report goes on, and on, and on . . . page after page after page . . . of admissions from practically everybody in the world that they just *do not know* how to do sex properly.

NOT ENOUGH OF IT

It has emerged from the report that the major reason people don't know how to do sex properly is that they don't get enough practice. Using the extensive computer facilities made available to her by the World Bank, and the latest computer graphics techniques, Ms Loud has been able to demonstrate how vast the problem is:

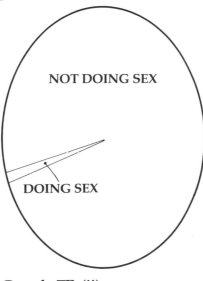

Graph 7B (ii)
Time spent doing sex

ABOUT THIS BOOK

Now that this terrible state of affairs has been exposed by the diligent work of the inquisitive Ms Loud, we believe it is time to publish the first ever book on *How To Do Sex Properly*.

As very few people know how to do it at all, our search for a team of experts who could break the vicious circle of ignorance was a very difficult task. But at last, after an extensive investigation and at great expense, we believe we have gathered together what must be, without doubt, the finest, most knowledgeable, most intelligent body of sexually experienced people in the world.

Between them they can notch up over 72 years of premarital sex (except Colin), 42 years of married sex (except Colin), 1 night of extra-marital sex (except Colin), and a great many children (except Colin). Colin knows a lot about teddy bears.

Signed: The Editors

HOW WILL SEX CHANGE ME?

Many people are worried that sex will change them in some way. It most certainly will, and in more ways than one. You cannot expect to undergo a deep emotional experience without some changes taking place.

WORRIED?

However, there is no need for you to worry about these. They are quite normal and happen to all of us. It will be easier to cope with these changes if you understand what is happening to you and your body at this time.

CRAZY HORMONES

Inside your body there are a lot of chemical messengers called "hormones". A deep emotional experience will disturb these hormones and they will start rushing around like crazy, playing havoc with various parts of the body as they go.

BODY HAIR

The first thing that you will notice is the growth of hair in places that used to be bald. This can be embarrassing for some people but, rest assured, it is very attractive to the opposite sex and some people consider it cuddly.

However, many people wish to remove these hairs because they prefer to have a bald body. This can be done by regular shaving or the use of one of the very good depilatory creams now on the market. A more permanent answer to the problem is removal by electrolysis.

GROWL

You will also notice that your voice becomes deeper, a growly tone replacing the high-pitched sounds made before the experience. When the voice starts to break like this some rather odd high and low sounds may come out of the mouth, but have no fear, soon a regular husky, growling voice will become established.

STUFFING

You will also find that you become very hungry after you have done it and you will eat a lot of food. Many people find they have a craving for pickles, or cold custard or even coal! This is called compulsive stuffing and is quite normal.

BIG TUM

Because of this compulsive stuffing you will find that your body shape changes considerably. The body "fills out", especially around the abdomen, arms and legs. You may have heard that it is possible "to knock the stuffing out" of someone, but unfortunately this is just an old wives' tale and you will have to put up with your new shape.

FLOPPY

Doing sex uses up a great deal of energy and may cause a feeling of fatigue and general floppiness. There will be long periods when a "changed" person will just sit, probably on the bed, staring, glassy-eyed, into space, with a silly grin on its face.

WHO TO DO IT WITH

Sex is not a pastime for the Loner (see Self-abuse, p44). In order to be able to do it properly you will need another person, and this person should be of a different sex from yourself, preferably the opposite one. It is important to know which physical attributes of the opposite sex you ought to be attracted by. These "parts", as they are called, may not initially interest you, but take encouragement from the fact that they have interested quite a lot of people in the past. If after lengthy study they still fail to interest you, there is probably something wrong with you.

THE IDEAL MALE

Points to watch for here are rippling muscles on chest, arms and thighs. It is quite alright for these parts to be hairy but Chuck here prefers to keep his chest bald and shiny so that the muscles glisten erotically in the sunlight. Some men appear to have breasts, which can be confusing (see opposite) but these are, in fact, well-developed muscles or, in some cases, fat.

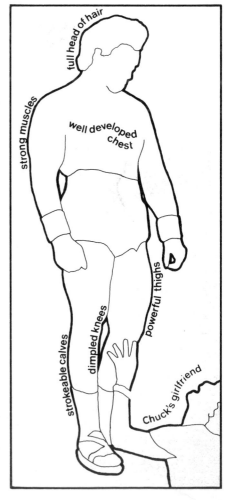

full head of hair

strong muscles

well developed chest

powerful thighs

dimpled knees

strokeable calves

Chuck's girlfriend

THE IDEAL FEMALE

Women carry two fleshy orbs which stick out the front. These are true "breasts" and should not be confused with big muscles. It is not alright if these parts are hairy. As a woman gets older, the two breasts gradually merge together into a single formation known as a "bosom".

To balance these protruberances and to prevent her toppling over forwards, a woman also has a rounded rear, or "bottom".

It is worth noting that whatever colour a woman's hair, the eyebrows should always be black.

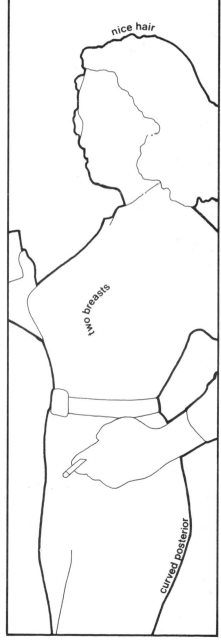

nice hair

two breasts

curved posterior

MAKING THE MOST OF YOURSELF

So now you know the sort of person you should be looking for to do sex with. Unfortunately this isn't going to help you very much if nobody wants to do sex with you. This is the time to take a good look at yourself in the mirror and consider – "Would I really want to do sex with that person?"

The answer is probably "No", but don't despair, there are many ways you can make yourself more attractive to the opposite sex.

First let's assess the magnitude of the problem that faces you. Remove your clothes and take another look in that mirror and what do you see – a miserable sloucher with round shoulders, sunken chest, flabby muscles, a pasty complexion, spotty skin, yellow teeth, red eyes? And what about that halitosis and B.O.?

It's obvious you're not going to get very far looking like this.

And that's not all. Sex is a very strenuous activity and you need to be fit and healthy to do it if you wish to avoid heart attacks, seizures, fits and shortage of breath. You need to be sure all your parts are in good working order before you start.

GOOD GROOMING

When it comes to sex, it is very important to have a well cared for appearance. If you look as though you don't care for yourself, how can you expect someone to care for you?

Here are a few tips to help you make the most of what you've got.

COPING WITH ACNE

Acne is not much fun. Those pimply pustules of dried grease put some people off and cause their owners a great deal of heartache. They are also impossible to cure.

And now for the good news. It is all a question of attitude. Don't sit alone sobbing in your room. If you can't get rid of your spots – make a feature of them.

Have you ever thought of turning them into beauty spots? Famous film stars have been doing it for years, so why not you?

Go out now and buy some black self-adhesive labels, cut them into tiny circles and stick them on your spots.

Never again will you have to lurk in dark corners trying to hide your face. From now on you will hold your head up high and
WEAR YOUR SPOTS WITH PRIDE.

TEETH

Yellow teeth and halitosis are going to put many potential partners off. Ordinary household bleach will remove the yellow stains but you still won't smell very nice. To cope with the halitosis and give you that extra allure, try adding Brut or Chanel No 5 to the soaking mixture.

EARWAX

Ears are very erogenous little zones that play a big part in sex. You can't see inside your own ears but never forget that other people can – groom them regularly.

GETTING HARD

Flaccid flesh is not very sexy. If yours hangs from your body, all loose and wrinkled, if it wobbles like jelly when you poke it, then you are going to have a lot of trouble finding someone to do sex with.

And even if you do find someone who is kinky about flab, you are still going to find that those wasted muscles are not really up to doing sex properly.

So here are a few exercises that will make you harder and increase your stamina for the strenuous activities that lie ahead.

WARNING: Do not attempt these exercises until you have had a full check-up from your doctor.

PRESS-UPS

Great training for sex. You may find when you reach position 4 that you cannot move. Ask your mother to call the doctor.

NOSE HAIRS

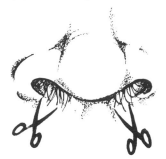

The trimming of nose hairs is a very tricky job. Using sharp little nail scissors, trim inside each nostril carefully. See also "nosebleeds".

EYEBALLS

Red eyeballs with large black bags under them are very sexy on Omar Sharif but they don't suit everybody. If you think yours are unattractive you have probably been using them too much, so the answer is to keep them closed. You could try lying on your back with a slice of lightly boiled eggplant on each eye – but it's not likely to make much difference.

FEET

Feet, unfortunately, have an intrinsic unattractiveness factor, so the only answer is to keep your socks on.

POSTURE

Good posture is essential for sex.

It makes you healthy, giving your heart and lungs plenty of room to work, and keeping your inside organs in their proper position for proper digestion, and so on. It is also very attractive to the opposite sex.

A slouching position, on the other hand, squashes all your organs and makes you generally weak and ill. Opposite sex people don't like it.

So whether standing or sitting – keep your chin up, shoulders back, and eyes forward.

HOW TO WALK PROPERLY

The right way   *Two very bad ways*

HOW TO SIT PROPERLY

The right way   *Two very bad ways*

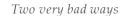

TOUCHING YOUR TOES

This is a tough one – it over-extends the knees at the back and exerts tremendous pressure on the lumbar vertebrae. Take Care.

DEEP KNEE BENDS

These over-extend the knee ligaments in the other direction and pinch the cartilage in the knee. A pair of crutches might be handy.

JOGGING

This will increase your stamina. It also shocks the vertebrae in the back causing degeneration of the spine, muscle spasm and herniated discs. With a force of nearly a quarter of a ton falling on to the foot, shin fractures are not unknown.

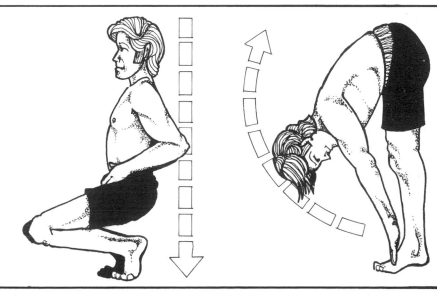

CONSTRUCT YOUR IDEAL PARTNER

We all have different ideas about our ideal partner.
Assembled here are all the possible parts you are likely to fancy. You merely have to choose the ones you like, glue them in the correct position on a piece of card, and carry your ideal person with you wherever you go. When you see the person that matches *your* ideal image, go up to it and ask it to do sex with you.

ARE YOU NORMAL?

Experts have concluded that many people are normal. No doubt you want to be normal too, and to help you find out about yourself we have included this questionnaire.

		A	B	C	Scores
1	**In a romantic situation do you stop at**	kissing	petting	nothing	**A** 6A 6C 10B 10A **B** 7A 7D 10B 10A **C** 10A 10B 7D 7A
2	**Do you prefer**	Hitler	Goering	Goebbels	**A** 16U 16V **B** 16U 17V **C** 17V 16U
3	**Does the opposite sex**	interest you	bore you	avoid you	**A** 14N 13O 14P 15O 14N **B** 14M 13N 14O 15N 14M **C** 13M 13O 15O 15M 13M
4	**Would you rather spend the evening with**	some rough soldiers	some nice sailors	some bishops	**A** 6P 9Q **B** 11K 11V **C** 13Q 16P
5	**Do you wear frilly panties**	often	always		**A** 7C 4E 2G 1J **B** 1J 2G 4E 7C
6	**You are invited to a fancy dress orgy. Do you go as**	Quasimodo	Tarzan	Snow White	**A** 11F 11H 9K 13K 11H **B** 11F 11H 10K 12K 11H **C** 11F 11G 9J 13J 11G
7	**Are you excited by handling**	fur	rubber	worms	**A** 4E 2D 1C **B** 4E 1E **C** 3F 1D
8	**You inadvertently stray onto a nudist beach. Do you pretend**	to be a reporter	to be blind	you're not interested	**A** 8N 7O 8P 9O 8N **B** 8M 7N 8O 9N 8M **C** 7M 7O 9O 9M 7M
9	**Do you find mud wrestling**	titillating	revolting	German	**A** 3S 2T 1T **B** 3S 3T 2U 1U **C** 7M 7O 9O 9M 7M
10	**Do you prefer your partner's chest to be**	hairy	bald		**A** 15C 18E 20G 21J **B** 21J 20G 18E 15C
11	**Should boy scouts be**	encouraged	tolerated	disciplined	**A** 6U 6V **B** 6U 5V **C** 5V 6U
12	**Do you wash behind your ears**	once a week	never		**A** 14V 16U 19S 21P **B** 21P 19S 16U 14V
13	**If you grow up do you want to be a**	gynaecologist	chiropodist	hairdresser	**A** 18E 20D 21C **B** 18E 21E **C** 19F 21D
14	**Who is President of the United States**	Sonny Tufts	Warner Baxter	Jeff Chandler	**A** 12A 12B 16C 16A **B** 12A 12B 15D 15A **C** 15A 15D 12B 12A
15	**Would you prefer to have**	acne	piles		**A** 9V 6U 3S 1P **B** 1P 3S 6U 9V
16	**Would you prefer to live in**	the town	the country	sin	**A** 19S 20T 21T **B** 19S 19T 20U 21U **C** 21U 20U 19T 19S
17	**How many uses can you think of for a toothbrush**	nine	twenty-one	two	**A** 11F 10E 8E 7H **B** 11F 9F 6J **C** 11F 9E 6H
18	**What did you pay for this book**	full price	half price	nothing	**A** 11F 12E 14E 15H **B** 11F 13E 16H **C** 11F 9E 6H

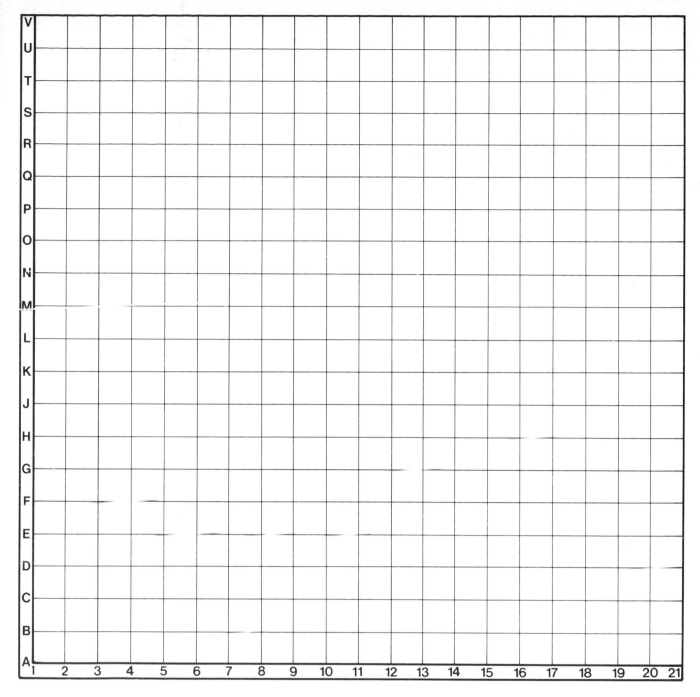

Answer the questions fearlessly. When you have chosen A, B, or C, join up the grid reference points given for that answer. Do this for every question to find out what sort of person you are.

PETER PAN

VAN GOGH

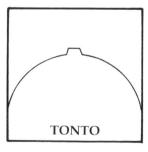

TONTO

HOW THE FAMOUS SCORED

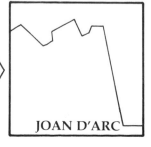

JOAN D'ARC

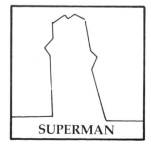

SUPERMAN

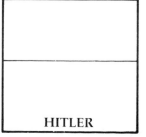

HITLER

LEARNING TO KISS RIGHT

Imagine that you have met a potential partner. Introductions are completed; you have shaken hands successfully. The next physical contact you will have to make is "the Kiss". It is very important that you get over this hurdle smoothly, as a bad kisser is unlikely to get much further down the slippery path to SEX.

can be open or closed

noses can be a problem, plastic surgery may help . . .

. . . tilting your head may suffice in mild cases

pressing too hard can cause bruising. Bathe in warm water. Use plenty of cold-cream

A Kiss is basically a touch with the mouth given by one person to another person, usually on his or her mouth. This is not as easy as it sounds.

Slobber can be quite a problem for the inexperienced kisser. Dribble tends to build up in the mouth during a kiss and it is important to dispose of this delicately and not let it run all over your partner's chin. For this reason it is better to do several short kisses rather than one long one, so that you have a chance to swallow the spittle or wipe it surreptitiously away on your partner's collar. A slobberer should always remember that kissing involves a sucking and not a blowing action.

You may have heard of some people talking about kissing with their mouths open. This is known as "the French Kiss" because it is said to be done by French people. We don't know very much about this but it doesn't sound very hygienic, does it? Perhaps it is alright for French people because all that garlic kills the microbes in their mouths.

But "what about intimate kissing?", we hear you ask. Well, this means kissing the "other bits" and is not everybody's cup of tea.

Make your own practice mouth by painting your hand with lipstick. Agitate the hand to imitate partner's urgent response.

*Try our kiss developer. If your nose is big it will get in the way so
cut along the dotted lines to provide nose aperture.*

EROGENOUS ZONES

These are the bits of the body that are supposed to like being prodded or rubbed when you are doing sex.

They are not at all easy to find, so study the drawings carefully and try to remember the important bits so you know what to look for when the big day comes.

Do not be rough when prodding these parts: start with a gentle poke and if this doesn't seem to have much effect, prod a bit harder until you get a response, such as "oooh" or "giggle, giggle".

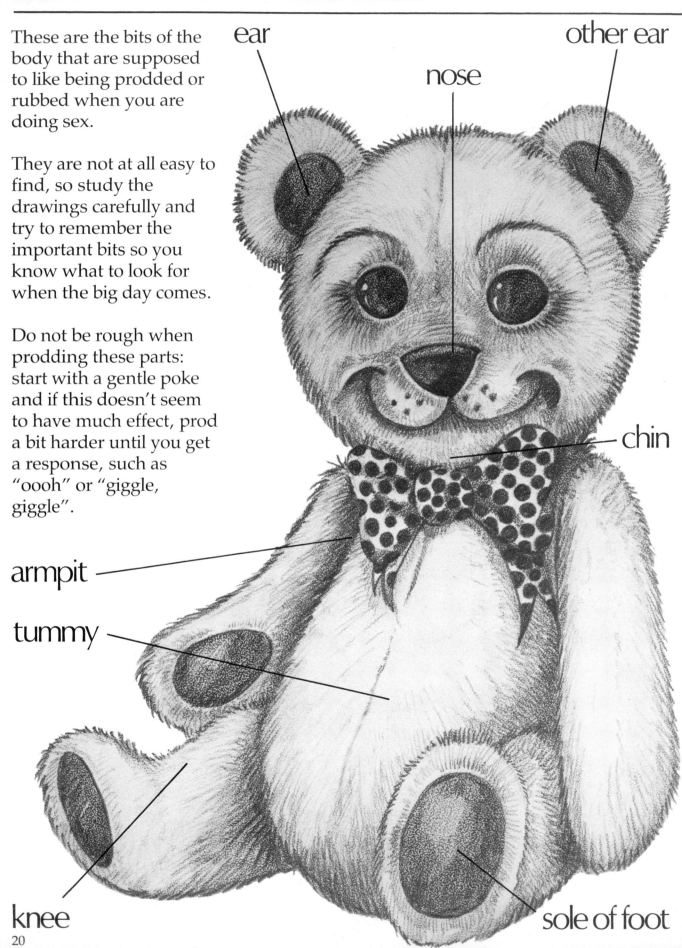

ear

nose

other ear

chin

armpit

tummy

knee

sole of foot

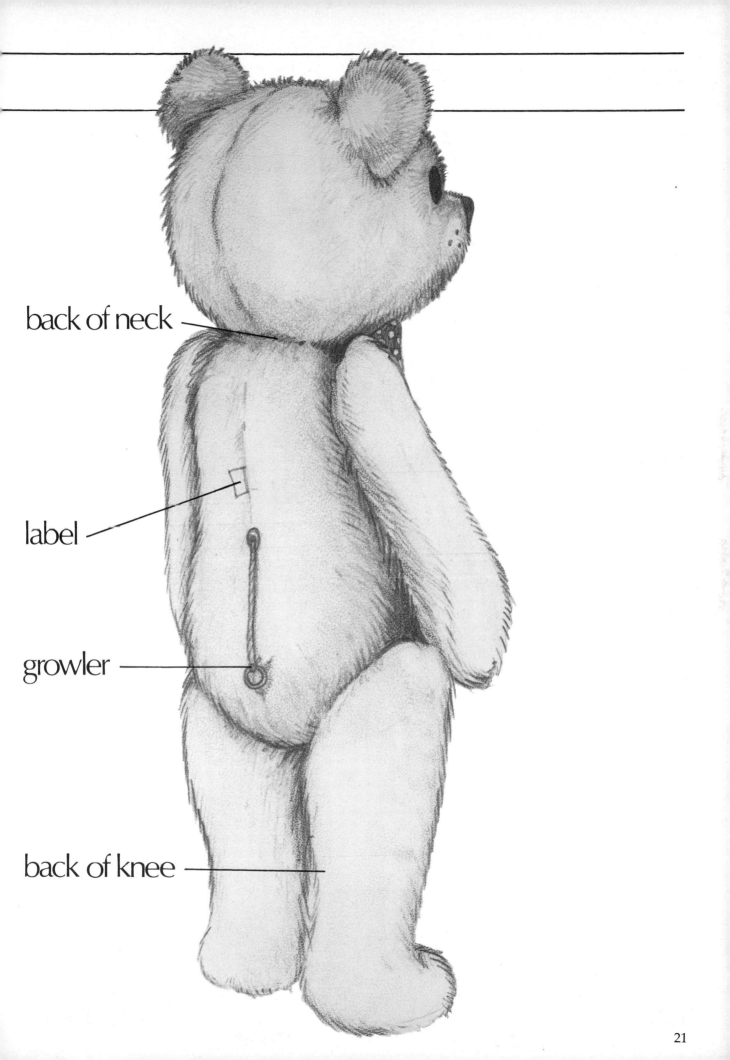

back of neck

label

growler

back of knee

FUMBLE-FREE UNDRESSING

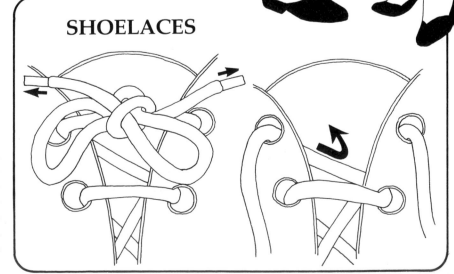

The removal of your clothes and those of your partner is one of the most important parts of the sexual act. There is nothing more off-putting than the fumbling of inexperienced fingers at button-holes, zippers and clasps.

The ability to undo and remove clothing while blinded by passion and hampered by the close proximity of another person is an art that must be learnt before you embark on a sexual career.

Practise undressing yourself with your eyes shut while standing extremely close to a wall or lying face down on the floor. Familiarize yourself with all the different types of garments you are likely to come across.

And when the big day comes for your first real encounter, remember to carry a small pair of scissors – just in case.

BUTTONS

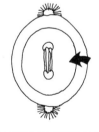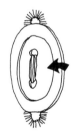

These little rascals are real fumble-traps. Beware of buttons that don't lead anywhere. A lot of valuable time can be wasted struggling with ornamental buttons, button-down collars, etc.

It is a good idea to take off shoes early in the operation as they can obstruct the removal of other garments. This often needs to be done with one hand while standing on one leg – a knack that requires highly developed manipulative skills and a good sense of balance.

SHOELACES

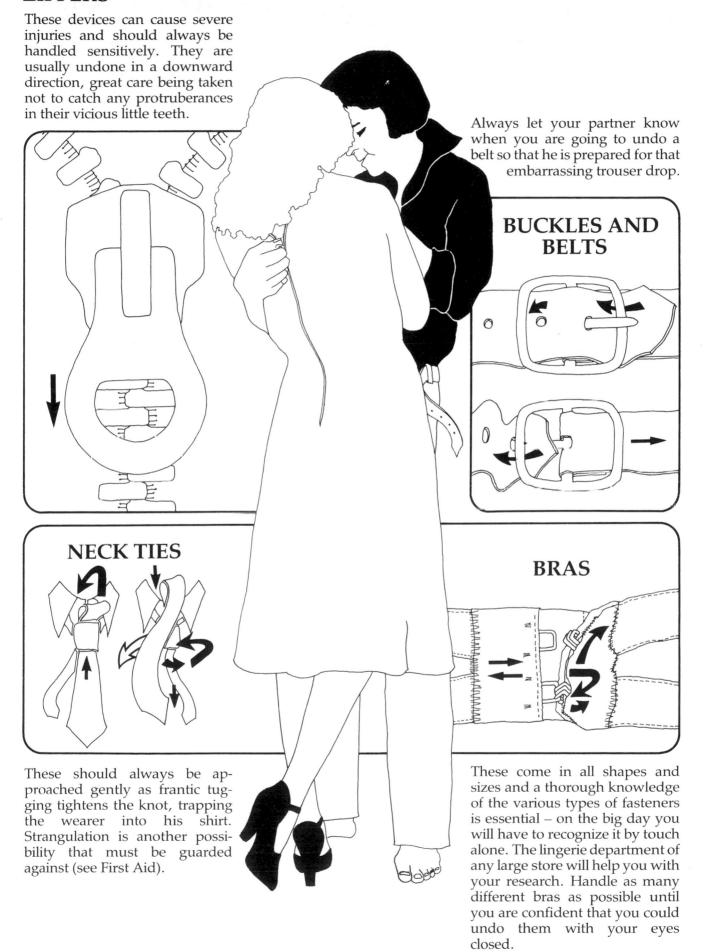

ZIPPERS

These devices can cause severe injuries and should always be handled sensitively. They are usually undone in a downward direction, great care being taken not to catch any protruberances in their vicious little teeth.

Always let your partner know when you are going to undo a belt so that he is prepared for that embarrassing trouser drop.

BUCKLES AND BELTS

NECK TIES

BRAS

These should always be approached gently as frantic tugging tightens the knot, trapping the wearer into his shirt. Strangulation is another possibility that must be guarded against (see First Aid).

These come in all shapes and sizes and a thorough knowledge of the various types of fasteners is essential – on the big day you will have to recognize it by touch alone. The lingerie department of any large store will help you with your research. Handle as many different bras as possible until you are confident that you could undo them with your eyes closed.

POSTURAL VARIATIONS

These are the positions you have to get into in order to do sex. They may look a little complicated but if you take the book to bed with you and follow the illustrations carefully you will soon get the hang of it. Remember to remove all sharp objects from your pockets and take off your spectacles before you begin.

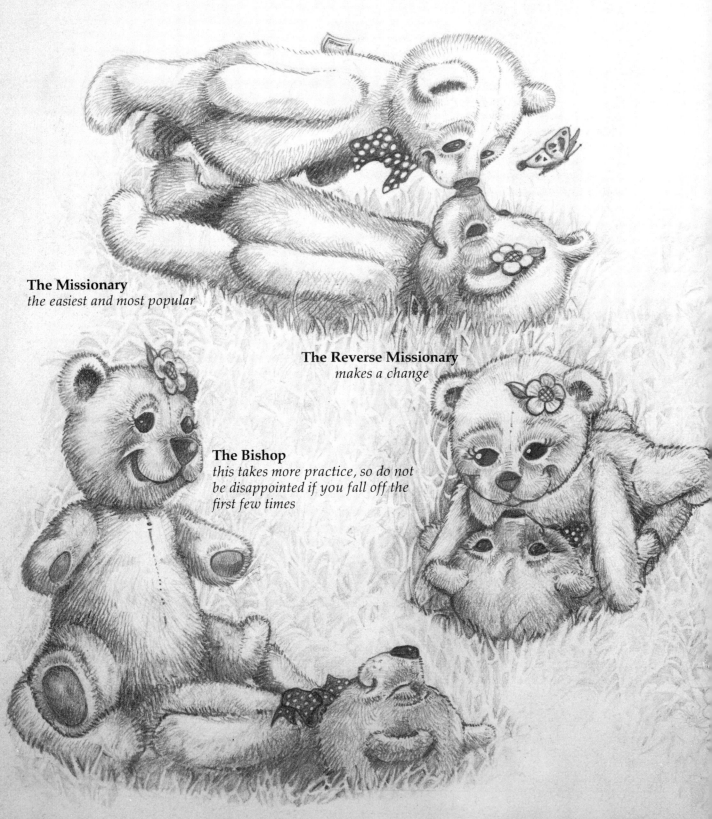

The Missionary
the easiest and most popular

The Reverse Missionary
makes a change

The Bishop
this takes more practice, so do not be disappointed if you fall off the first few times

The Australian
Bruce and Sheila show you how

The Octopus
lots of fun

BODY LANGUAGE

Body language is the way people move, behave and look. People of different nations and races have different body languages, and it is by recognizing a person's body language that you can tell what language that person speaks.

The North American

Speaks a version of English known as American (not to be confused with French Canadian which is quite different). If you speak any version of English you should find American fairly easy to understand, especially as it is usually spoken rather loud.

Unless "your" American has spent a lot of time in California it will probably be at its best doing something straightforward, but watch out for regional variations.
VERDICT: Fairly safe, well fed.

The French

Speaks French, which is still taught in some schools but which is very difficult to do well. Will not speak any other language even if it knows it, and will laugh at your efforts.

All this is a bad start, but it gets worse: the French thinks it is a superb sexual performer, which by Belgian standards it may be, and it will probably be keen on exotic activities accompanied by lots of wine, extravagant ges-tures and garlic odours.
VERDICT: Could be interesting but who needs it?

The German

Speaks a language which few bother to learn and which involves a lot of throaty noises and some spitting. Do not be too put off by this. The German has a long and impressive cultural history and is really a nice person,

calm and friendly, but when it gets overexcited all hell breaks loose. This is often caused by drinking too much *Bier* (beer) or *Schnapps* (whatever that is), or a combination of both. In these circumstances be prepared for some heavy stuff, e.g. bondage, whips, vomiting, domination.
VERDICT: Play this one to suit your mood. At worst, unlikely to be fatal.

The Japanese
Here's a puzzle. These ones are everywhere but are usually seen in large groups all talking simultaneously. You do not speak the language but as you are unlikely to find a Japanese on its own this may not matter. Not much is known about the Japanese but it does like rituals and ceremonies, also suicide. So the possibilities

would seem to be (a) group sex, (b) ceremonial sex, and (c) terminal sex.
VERDICT: Small but vigorous. Do at least *try* to find out which of the above variations your Japanese is interested in.

The British
Speaks a version of English now not widely understood. The Scottish is not understood at all. Considered to be enigmatic and reserved, the British is actually inspirational, highly talented, perfectly formed and extrovert. The British is a creative and sym-

pathetic partner in love. Unfortunately it considers itself superior in most respects to other peoples, which it probably is not – but it has to be treated as if it is, if it is to give of it best.
VERDICT: Dull, not even very reliable.

The Australian
Extensively modified form of English spoken, not taught in schools even in its homeland. Makes itself understood in any language by noisy, boisterous behaviour. Very strong interest in sex due to scarcity of people, excess of sheep, in its continent. The Australian favours the direct approach and is a hearty partner but uses a lot of bad language, which is not meant to offend.
VERDICT: Sensitive, retiring, full of surprises.

IT PAYS TO ADVERTISE

You should now have some idea of the basic theory of how to do sex. It is now time to practise what you have learnt so far.

To do this you will need an opposite sex person to practise on. It is not always easy to find one of these. It is not a good idea to just go up to one and ask it if you can do sex with it. This approach usually ends in failure and can lead to bruises and abrasions (see First Aid).

If you wish to avoid these mishaps, it is very important to be sure that the opposite sex person you approach also wants to practise. One way to find such a person, with little risk to yourself, is to advertise for it.

Now, advertising is almost as difficult as sex, which is why advertising executives are paid so much. For this reason it is probably better to start by answering other people's advertisements until you have got the hang of the "jargon".

"Jargon" is necessary because every word costs money and so the advertiser has to give as much information as possible in the fewest possible words. For this reason you have to read the advertisements very carefully to find out if the advertiser is really the sort of person you are looking for.

The following are a few typical examples of the advertisements you are likely to come across, accompanied by an explanation from our expert – Miss Constance Loving, proprietress of the Constance Loving Introduction and Colonic Irrigation Bureau. Study them carefully before you answer any ads in your local paper.

Well-bred young lady seeks stable relationship.

This sort of thing is quite common among well-bred young ladies. They tend to get bored with well-bred young men and often yearn for stable lads and jockeys. This would be a good opportunity for a young man who likes working with horses.

Gay guy seeks soul-mate for meaningful relationship.

This young man has led a very gay life and has never had time to form a deep relationship. He needs a sympathetic and loving woman to bring some stability into his life.

Dave, 37, shy, isolated, needs sympathetic, understanding girlfriend. Interests: jazz, socialism, personal growth, and discovering what it's all about.

Poor Dave has problems. He is unlikely to get any bigger at his age and his smallness has obviously made him take up some rather subversive hobbies. Still, he does want to discover what sex is all about, and if you're desperate and very small he might do.

Second-hand chest of drawers for sale. Needs stripping.

Beware of advertisments like this. There are unscrupulous people around who slip rude words like "chest" and "drawers" into their advertisements to lure unsuspecting people into their houses for immoral purposes. They are so devious that they often advertise in the "For Sale" columns of their local paper in order to escape the notice of the vice squad.

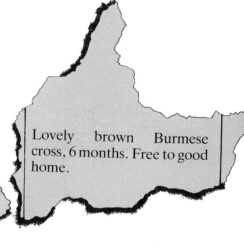

Lovely brown Burmese cross, 6 months. Free to good home.

Oriental ladies are always a good choice. This lovely young lady lady is free of any romantic attachments but unfortunately has been rather cross lately, probably because she has not got a good home. I am sure she would respond to love and affection and make a co-operative partner.

Composing Your Own Advertisements

Constance Loving advises:

If none of the advertisements you answer produces the desired results, then you will be forced to place your own advertisement.

The first thing to decide is how much you want to spend. Take a tip from me. The less spent the better, because usually the less said the better.

Fortunately the vocabulary of Lonely Hearts Advertising is very small, and I list below all the words you will ever need. Just choose the ones you like the best and make your very own Lonely Hearts Ad.

How to Do It

Choose as many words from Column A as you like and put them in Box 1. Put a word from Column B in Box 2. Then some more A words in Box 3 and a B word in Box 4. Finally, put a C word in Box 5. And that's all there is to it.

For example:
Petite, dusky
Frenchman
seeks
gay, single-parent, disabled
plumber
for
photographic modelling

| 1 | 2 | SEEKS | 3 |
| 4 | FOR | 5 |

> Super young chick wanted by fantastically wealthy farmer. Must be outstanding for outstanding offer.

I am not quite sure why this gentleman is advertising in a lonely hearts column, it is probably a mistake. However, rich chicken farmers can make good partners and he might worth contacting.

> Strict young French mistress. Available by the hour. Ask for Fifi.

French is a very useful language when travelling in France and some parts of Belgium. You may even strike up a relationship with a French person. French people know how to do sex properly.

> Experience our lovely underwear. Everything half price this week at Frederick's of Hollywood.

If you are really desperate, then you may have to pay for it. Look out for special offers like this.

A	B	C
Curvaceous	bachelor (girl)	good time
well-endowed	widow(er)	foreign travel
brawny	divorce(e)	shopping trips
strapping	mother-of-three	discipline
ample	guy	bareback riding
petite	chick	Egyptian PT
slim	model	unnatural practices
svelte	Tarzan/Jane	meaningful relationship
gay	plumber	photographic modelling
funloving	Frenchman	canoeing
go-getting	chiropodist	penetrating conversations
shy	bank manager	arm wrestling
lonely	student	educational visits
retiring	nudist	deep-sea diving
attractive	weightlifter	mystical experiences
homely	executive	exciting activities
disabled	steeplejack	nights of passion
single-parent	grandfather/mother	keep fit exercises
dusky	eskimo	sex

questionnaire

So that our computer can fix you up with your ideal partner we first need to collect some information about you and your preferences. Please read each question carefully and tick (√) the box against the correct answer.

All of these people are in our computer. Tick the one you want to do sex with.

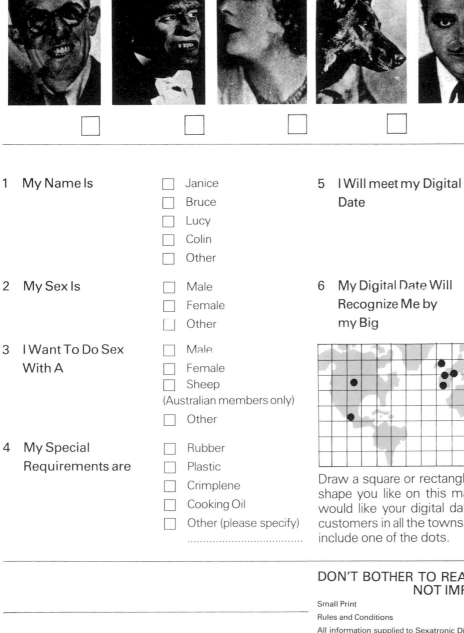

☐	☐ ☐ ☐ ☐ ☐

1 My Name Is
☐ Janice
☐ Bruce
☐ Lucy
☐ Colin
☐ Other

2 My Sex Is
☐ Male
☐ Female
☐ Other

3 I Want To Do Sex With A
☐ Male
☐ Female
☐ Sheep (Australian members only)
☐ Other

4 My Special Requirements are
☐ Rubber
☐ Plastic
☐ Crimplene
☐ Cooking Oil
☐ Other (please specify)
....

5 I Will meet my Digital Date
☐ Under the clock
☐ Outside Tesco's
☐ In the public lavatory
☐ Elsewhere

6 My Digital Date Will Recognize Me by my Big
☐ Nose
☐ Feet
☐ Other Thing

Draw a square or rectangle or circle or triangle or any shape you like on this map to indicate the area you would like your digital date to come from. We have customers in all the towns marked on the map so try to include one of the dots.

_____

_____

_____

_____

My Credit Card Number Is ☐☐☐☐☐☐☐☐

the People who want to do Sex

CORRESPONDENCE COURSE

After finding an attractive member of the opposite sex there may be some delay before achieving your ultimate goal. There may even be a time when you are apart and need to correspond. Rather than a setback, this could prove to be the making of your venture if you comply with the "Romantic Rules".

To Barbara - my light, my delight

The moon shines bright
For our lovers tryst
Our arms embrace
For the times we missed
I whisper gently
I love you
You drink champagne
from my Blue suede shoe
Your Bobby socks
My bootlace tie
Your pleated skirt
My black hair dye

These things make us
the perfect duo
Its fate my dear that
I love yuo

To the one I hold most dear, in estimation of my undying love for you I forward the first lines of my most recent sonnet:

But soft! what light through yonder window breaks?
It is the east, and Gladys is the sun.

I continue to write and in person will recite the completed work at our next tryst

your affectionate

Charles xxxxx

I WANT YOU!

yours sincerely
R. Wainright (Esq.)

Miss Denning
Cactus Cottage
Charlestown
New South Wales
AUSTRALIA

Rule 1
Always use a typewriter, with no handwriting to positively identify you. Disclaiming authorship is always possible in an emergency.

Rule 2
Poetry is difficult – avoid it.

Rule 3
If you must write poetry, borrowing inspiration could have a deleterious effect and may not sound as good as the original anyway.

Rule 4
Subtlety is as important as politeness.

Dear Martin

I'm writing on behalf of Sarah who is in hospital right now. The doctors say she'll be alright but her left thumb is missing and no-one can find it anywhere (what a mystery).

Enclosed is a package, addressed to you, which was found next to her writing table, I thought it might be important! Hope you'll be able to visit her in hospital as soon as possible, I'm sure

P.T.O.

P.T.O.

Rule 5
Writing in blood may seem a good idea to prove your sincerity, but clotting in the pen and dizziness may adversely affect you judgement.
If you feel this is a necessity then tomato ketchup will look just as good (and smell better).

Rule 6
Don't commit yourself.

▼

For You I'd Climb the highest mountain wade the deepest river, swim the coldest lake, dive naked from the highest cliff, fight the fiercest army, leap the widest chasm, descend the deepest cave, hold my breath for ever, cut off all my hair, starve myself for months on end, tie my legs in knots, wiggle my ears, pull funny faces, cut off an arm, listen to your Dean Martin records, pierce my ears, fight a boa constrictor, rob a bank, learn to cook and I'd even, yes even, wash the dishes!

yours truly
Sheila Willcox

Dear Robin,

My body throbs for you constantly, I lay awake at night unable to dispell the thought of your cool strong body next to mine, your gentle touch, your soft caress, these are desires I can no longer resist.

My darling, I need you, I want you, I cannot live without your vibrant passion, your tireless embrace, your eager kisses, the rapture of a night

spent in your arms. Come to me as soon as possible, be with me, release me from my prison of lonliness, break my bonds of solitude and delight me with your love in the warmth of our privacy.

waiting and counting each second till your arrival

Deidre

p.s. phone first in case I'm busy.

Rule 7
Some good groundwork can be laid with the right kind of subtle communication, but beware, a casual comment can ruin the most carefully prepared love letter.

WHAT WENT WRONG?

If you have studied this book of instruction you will know how to do sex properly. However, before you proceed further you should know that in sex, as in every other aspect of life, practically everything that can go wrong does go wrong.

You should be prepared for disappointment, embarrassment and distress, also a certain amount of physical pain, ranging from grazes and contusions to ruptures and splintered bones.

We are not unaware, as are many so-called experts in this field, of the unexpected problems that can, and do, arise when attempting to do sex. However, with knowledge and forethought many of the worst disasters can be mitigated, if not entirely avoided.

YOUR SEXUAL DISASTER CHART
Diagnosis and Remedy

Problem	Symptoms	Possible causes	Remedy
Lack of oxygen	Inability to breathe; dizziness; fainting; death	Your bedclothes have worked their way over your head	*If you are conscious:* Push the bedclothes back and take some deep breaths
		Your partner's ample flesh is blocking your breathing orifices	Change your position or your ample partner
		You have forgotten to keep breathing	Start breathing again
			If you are unconscious: Put your head between your knees or raise your feet *If you appear to be dead:* Ask your partner to give you the kiss of life or a heart massage
Sweat, excess of	You body loses its grip, slips and slides all over the place; distressing rude noises when attempt made to release suction effect of moisture	Too many clothes or bedclothes Over enthusiastic activity Hot nights	Remove your socks and thermal underwear; reduce the tog rating of your duvet Calm down, take it slower Don't do it on hot nights

Problem	Symptoms	Possible causes	Remedy
Slobber, excess of	Wet pillow; hot wet feeling on your/ your partner's cheeks and trickling into your/your partner's ears	Failure to swallow enough Too long kisses You/your partner is just a slobbery person	Swallow regularly Do shorter kisses Pack your/your partner's cheeks with an absorbant material
Excruciating Pain	Excruciating Pain	There is a foreign object on the bed/rug/beach/ dashboard/kitchen table digging into you Your partner is too heavy Your partner is kneeling on your hair Your partner has its elbow in your groin Your partner has broken your leg	Change your position, taking care not to disturb anything, especially your broken leg
		Cramp, rheumatism	Put corks down your bed; potato peelings under your pillow and wear thermal underwear (*see also* Sweat, excess of)
		You are having a heart attack	Ask your partner to put you in the recovery position (*see* First Aid) and call the doctor
Off-putting Noises	The occurrence of strange sounds that put you/your partner off your/ its stroke	The bed is squeaking Excess of sweat Excess of "wind" Excess of passion Ghosts	Oil the springs or do it somewhere else *See* Sweat, excess of Wait for the wind to die down Light up a cigarette Call your local exorcist
Embarrassment, wanting to die of	Hot flushes Feelings of shame Unwillingness to remove clothing	There is something very wrong with part of your/your partner's body	Draw the curtains Turn the lights off Plastic surgery
Absence of Pleasure	Boredom	You/your partner is doing something wrong	Read this book again carefully. Are you putting everything in the right place?
		You/your partner is doing everything right, but you just don't like sex	Don't worry, there are a lot of other interesting activities you can take up

EMERGENCY ACTION

If you haven't learnt how to do sex properly and you do it all wrong, you may find yourself in a situation that calls for emergency action. You must be prepared to act quickly and it is important to know the correct procedure for (a) choking, (b) fainting, (c) the kiss of life, (d) cardiac arrest, (e) the Holger-Nielson Method, (f) recovery.

(a)

GRAB YOUR VICTIM

Stand close behind her encircling her with your arms and give a hard upward thrust into her abdomen.

(b)

UNDO CLOTHING

Undo all tight clothing as fast as possible.

(c)

MOUTH TO MOUTH

Position the victim and cover her mouth with your lips and blow.

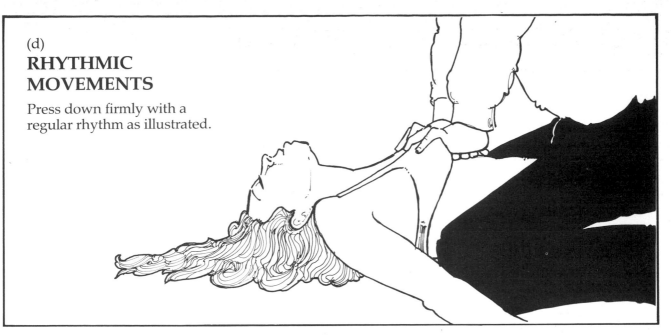

(d)
RHYTHMIC MOVEMENTS

Press down firmly with a regular rhythm as illustrated.

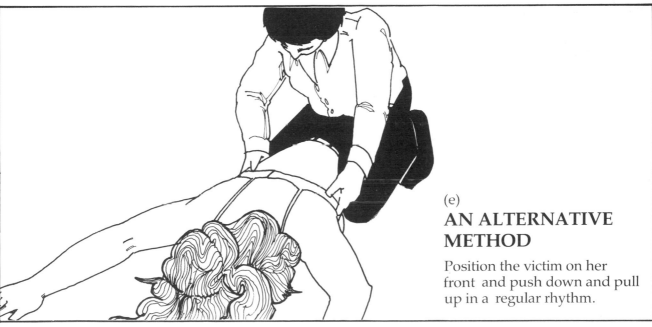

(e)
AN ALTERNATIVE METHOD

Position the victim on her front and push down and pull up in a regular rhythm.

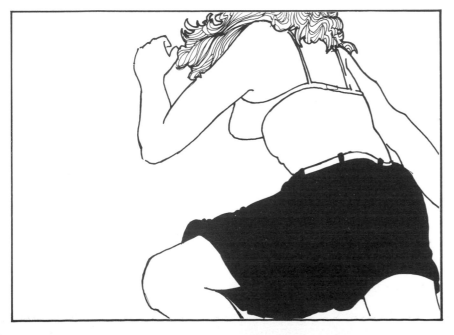

(f)
RECOVERY

When your victim has stopped choking, regained consciousness, started breathing or resumes a regular heartbeat, leave her in the recovery position.

THE PERILS OF PARTY TIME

A Mating Game
for up to 23 players

Aim of the Game

To construct an ongoing ballpark analysis model of socio-sexual parameters in ambigendrous ritual partytime encounter situations

And

go to bed with an attractive person.

How to Play

1 Look in all the usual places for dice, e.g. kitchen drawer, and down back of couch, raincoat pocket, dog's bed.

2 Agree on rules.

3 Decide who goes first.

4 Turns pass anti-clockwise left to right and vice versa.

5 Play continues ad nauseam.

Rules

1 No spitting.

2 Rules may not be invented retrospectively.

3 No cheating.

4 Players may not interfere with each other (much) until bedroom is reached.

5 First player to reach the bedroom waits until he/she is joined by another player. These two may then leave the room.

START
Throw a one to select your target.

Meeting of eyes across room. move on 3 squares.

Knock over Priceless Antique Throw again

Eat too many Pickled Onions move back 3 squares

Even No: Suggest somewhere quieter. move on 3 squares

Odd No: Asthma attack move back 3 squares

Wig comes off in struggle go back 3 squares

Queue for buffet. miss 1 turn and move on one square.

Odd No: Target wants to eat Food

Even No: Wants to eat you move on 3 squares

Have Drunk too much, Start again after you miss 2 turns

Loosen more clothing and sweat next turn eagerly

Odd No: Go to sleep for rest of Party.

Even no: Room occupied follow finger

DO NOT DISTURB

BREAK WIND miss one turn

Dance until next turn

Bump into old schoolfriend. Miss 1 turn.

Visit Bathroom Zipper stuck call help. go to square 5

Odd No: Target admires your mind more than your body. go back 2 squares
Even No: You fall asleep, move on 2 squares

Odd No: Heavy breathing and move on 7 squares.
Even No: Their Spouse appears. Start again.

3 Visit Bathroom. Miss 1 turn

☆ Even No: Target admires Tan. move on 2 squares

Odd No: You Have Halitosis. go back 1 square.

5 Host/Hostess finds you wildly exciting

☆ Even No: Target accepts drink move on 3 squares

Odd No: Spill Drink on Target go back 4 squares.

Host/Hostess circulating with drinks take 1 and move on 3

Discover Target's in drag — remember urgent appointment

Even No: Mild petting till next turn

Odd No: Not mutual go back to square 1

Host/Hostess introduces you to party bore throw 8 1 to escape.

You introduce bore to target. go back 2 squares.

Ice well & truly broken move on three squares

Target collapses in helpless laughter and asks for a drink

☆ Even No: Target downs drink and wants another move on 4 squares.

Odd No: Target downs drink and wants the bottle. move on 2 squares.

Cat mounts wig throw 1 or 2 to proceed

Host/Hostess returns to rescue you. go back 5 squares

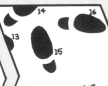

Dance until you throw 8 4 or more.

Vomit unexpectedly Go back to square 3

☆ Even No: Wants to dance move on 5 squares

Odd No: Target wants to eat go back 5 squares.

Turn conversation to Hite/Kinsey/Freud

Have an extra turn

Even No: Happy not to talk - follow the finger.

Odd No: Downs drink and talks incessantly move on 3

12 Nobody finds you interesting sneak out of party.

Odd No: Target starts to loosen your clothing move on 4

Even No: Share bottle Advance 5 squares

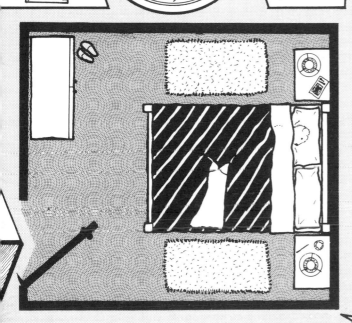

39

CAUGHT IN THE ACT

A. **Outside on ledge.** You should first have checked there is a ledge.

B. **Hanging from ledge.** Not recommended for long periods.

C. **Under rug.** Try not to sneeze.

D. **In chest.** Ensure your air supply.

E. **Under the bed.** Measure spring clearance.

F. **On bed canopy.** If adequately supported.

G. **Hanging from chandelier.** Difficult to get away with.

or COITUS INTERRUPTUS

If you attempt "illegal" sex, you may find that your coitus is interrupted. On these occasions it will be necessary to find a good hiding place. It is advisable to check out the possibilities before you commit yourself.

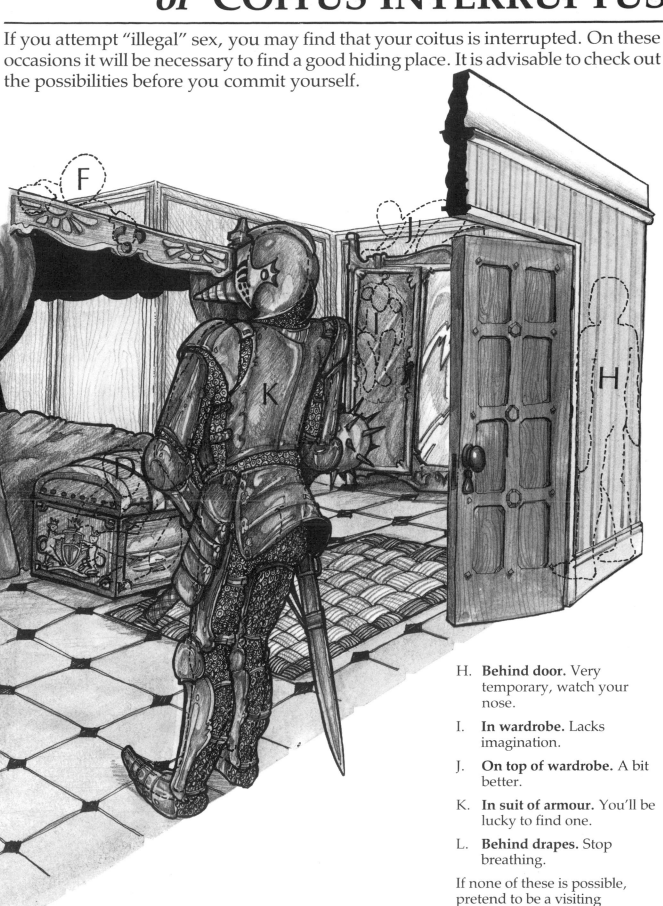

H. **Behind door.** Very temporary, watch your nose.

I. **In wardrobe.** Lacks imagination.

J. **On top of wardrobe.** A bit better.

K. **In suit of armour.** You'll be lucky to find one.

L. **Behind drapes.** Stop breathing.

If none of these is possible, pretend to be a visiting acupuncturist, masseur, faith healer or tax inspector.

FETISHES AND DEVIATIONS

These are a good idea when things start to get boring, but they can be habit-forming and some are a bit uncomfortable. As some of the outfits and equipment involved can be costly, it's worth having a trial run with borrowed items before you decide to make the investment. Even then, don't forget to study the small ads in your local paper for secondhand outfits – this could also lead to contacts with others who share your interests.

Wearing Ladies' Clothing (men only)

Quite an economical one unless you have to buy outsize or made-to-measure. Best to go for bright colours and plenty of dainty frills to draw attention away from your hairy arms and legs. Fishnet stockings are fun but not very warm. Experiment with make-up and high heels before "going public".

Rubberwear

This is rather expensive unless you are prepared to settle for cut-price Far Eastern imports. There are lots of rubberwear enthusiasts and you will probably find there is a social club in your district where you can go for a coffee and a chat.

We suggest you use plenty of deodorant and talc, though true devotees rather frown on these. For extra interest you can wear flippers and a mask, though you will need to learn to breathe without this misting up – and remember that flippers don't look right with socks.

Finally, BE CAREFUL when you use the full-length zipper.

Bondage

A growing sport all about tying other people up or being tied up yourself. Chains seem to be more popular than rope, while string and sticky tape are definitely out. It may seem like fun but some people do get terribly overexcited when doing bondage and this means they can be very rough and hurt you quite a lot. If you like being hurt a lot then you will be happy – and of course you can hurt them back when it's your turn.

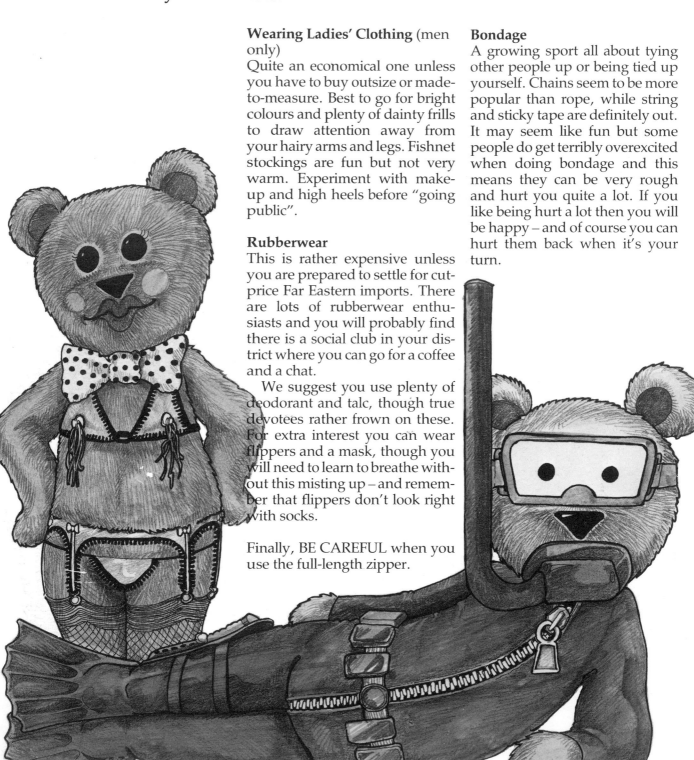

As for equipment, you can get by on about 30 feet of stainless steel 1½ inch chain and a pair of handcuffs (easily picked up at your next police garage sale).

Exposing Yourself

Otherwise known as "flashing", this involves going about without your knickers on and, as the mood takes you, showing your most intimate bits to strangers. At first this will cause you deep embarrassment, especially if you have by mistake forgotten to remove your knickers, but then it is very cheap and you do get to meet a lot of people.

Whips and Boots

If you are the sort of person who likes TV costume dramas then this one is for you. It simply *breathes* history and has a really strong period flavour. Try to get in with a crowd who use the whips for atmosphere rather than for real if you don't like pain. Lots of opportunities for dressing up and for using old-fashioned language like "Forsooth", "Sirra", etc. If you do a good Marquis de Sade impression you'll go down really well, while girls are always a success in naughty riding gear with a cheeky little cocked hat, a Lone Ranger mask, and a beauty spot.

THE PROBLEM OF SELF-ABUSE

This can be quite a problem. Now I am not going to go into details – let us just say that it is a temptation that is pretty sure to come to you at one time or another and I want to warn you against it.

A Dirty Beast

A Healthy Lad

NASTY HABIT

I expect there are a lot of you who will be glad of a word of advice against this nasty habit which gets hold of so many chaps and girls today. It is sometimes called beastliness, and that is about the best word for it.

Now beastliness is not a good show. It has caused most of the poor eyesight we see around today. There is no way you can get into the army if you haven't got 20/20 vision – think about that.

PIMPLES

Dry, lifeless, unmanageable hair, baldness, spots and pimples, knock knees, flat feet, ingrown toenails, bunions, protruding ears – these are just some of the *outward* signs of this secret vice, or sickness – for have no doubt, that is what it is, the result of an impure mind and tainted blood. There are also *internal* manifestations. It retards growth, dulls the brain and fills the mind with disgusting ideas. Cowardice is a striking peculiarity of the "beast" – he cannot look a person full in the face.

STOP IT

Now I expect you are all saying to yourselves "how do I stop it?" Well, I'll tell you. First you have to know the cause.

The basic cause is DIRT. If you have got dirty blood, you will get a dirty mind and vice versa. It is all joined up, you see.

Now, dirt clogs the system and makes the blood hot, so the first thing to do is to check how dirty you are by taking your temperature.

TESTING FOR DIRT

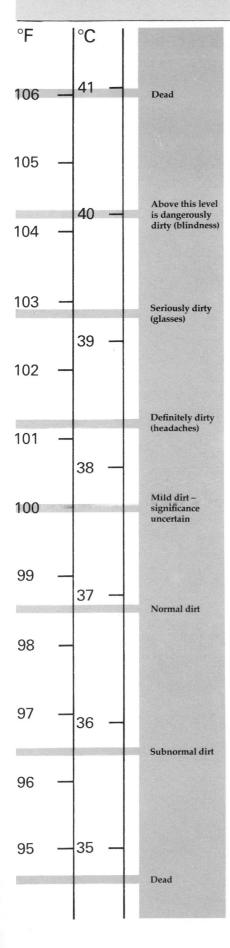

1. Take a firm grip of the top between the fingers and thumb.
2. Hold it away from the body (and anything else).
3. Bend forearm up at the elbow.
4. Rapidly straighten arm right down.
5. Immediately, without stopping, give a hard jerking flick of the hand at the wrist.

If possible work well above a soft surface (eg bedclothes) so that you hit nothing and risk little if you let go. Now put it in your mouth, leave it for one minute and then take it out and have a look at it.

You will probably find it is well above normal. So now you have found just how dirty you are, how do you clean yourself up?

TRASH
Well, I expect you all like to listen to dirty stories, read trashy books and look at lewd pictures. You think you get pleasure from such pastimes, but bear in mind that these things are bound to lead you into the temptation of self-abuse or beastliness. This is a most dangerous thing, for it quickly becomes a habit and will destroy your health and spirits and you will never be much good.

SILLY FOOLS
If you want to be strong and healthy you will throw off such temptations at once; you will stop looking at the books and pictures; you will say to your friends "you are silly fools and I will not listen to your filth". You will give yourself something else to think about – something clean and pure, like your mother, or your sister.

FLUSH IT OUT
All these things will help, but you must also attack the problem of your dirty blood. There are three points to remember here:

1. you should not let dirty things get into your blood;
2. when they get in, you should flush them out;
3. keep your blood cool.

BOILED COD
Sometimes the desire is brought on by indigestion caused by too much rich food. It can therefore be cured by correcting this. A diet of boiled cod, steamed spinach and mashed turnip is recommended.

DIRTY MATTER
It is also essential to clear out all dirty matter from the inside of your stomach, which is done by "going to the rear" every day, without fail; many people are better off for doing it twice a day. If you have any difficulty about it one day, drink plenty of hot water and jump up and down on the spot for half an hour and all should be well.

UNHEALTHY PRACTICES
"Bad" dreams are another cause of the trouble. These are sometimes caused by sleeping on your back, or more usually by hot blood due to sleeping with too many blankets on or in too warm a room. Try to avoid these unhealthy practices, but if you still have trouble jump straight into a cold bath and exercise the *upper* half of your body vigorously.

DO IT ONCE
You will probably find it difficult to overcome these temptations the first time you try, but when you have done it once it will be easier afterwards. You can be sure that if you follow my advice all will come right. And always remember the three Cs of Continence: Clean mind
Cold baths
Cool blood.

THE FACTS OF LIFE

CINDY AND ELAINE ARE ON THE BEACH...

EROTIC FANTASIES

Many people find it difficult to do sex unless they are in a romantic frame of mind. This is possibly some deep-rooted instinct left over from bygone days when sex and romance were believed to be linked. Unfortunately, romance is much too expensive and time-consuming to be practised these days.

However, do not despair – all you have to do is to conjure up an erotic fantasy. Erotic fantasies not only help you to get in the right frame of mind to do sex, they can even replace sex altogether. In fact, they are really a lot better than the real thing.

You can have them when and where you want, any time of the day or night, and they're free!

So here's an idea to get you started – one for guys and one for gals.

A.

You are a mousy little typist with a boring job in a big office. You are walking home from work one day when a huge camel races up behind you bearing a delicious-looking arab who drags you on to his camel and takes you back to his tent in the desert where he showers you with jewels and sheep's eyes and things . . . etc.

B.

You are an impoverished little arab who suddenly inherits your long-lost uncle's oil wells, jewels, camels and things. You are riding along on your camel one day when you come across a beautiful blonde typist walking along the road. You grab her and take her back to your tent in the desert where you shower her with jewels, ice cream, oil and things . . . etc.

Try it once and you'll be amazed how it gets a grip on you!

SEX: a psychologist explains

Man's raison d'être in this world is to make and keep things as pleasant as possible, a view circumcized to by Freud. Freud felt that every sexual act was motivated by the emergence of two basic positions; firstly, a mutual desire for pleasure and, secondly, a natural desire for avoidance of pain. It was identification with the latter which led to a variety of other positions being developed.

WHIPPED

Hysterically, there were those who did not possess either the strength or determination to push a new approach through and as a result they could not accept any interpretation which suggested a wasting of time by analyzing those factors said to be inbedded in sex. The climax of their argument came with Freud's insistence that sex was a complex function. By stating that the whole act was tied up with a need to go for a drive of some sort, he whipped up a state of fury which put the cap on productive thinking and served to act as an effective contraception to any additional explorations.

Anti-Freudians pointed to the humble amoeba as a perfect model – they weren't complex. It was noted that by parting they were starting sex, something they seemed to be able to manage without too much difficulty, so why not able-bodied primates? Sex was not the insurmountable problem which was being implied. It was argued that the outstanding characteristics of the conscious mind are its active processes, not its passive contents. In other words, how could either you or your partner have a satisfying sexual relationship when you were asleep; who, apart from those who had a castration complex, wanted just to dream about sex?

HELLO SAILOR

The "Electra" complex, which Freud said operates in the female unconscious, was viewed by many a flushed and excited spinster as being shocking, while the "Oedipus" complex led to a line of thought, particularly amongst those voyeurs at sea, which eventually came up with the startling conclusion that there were indeed profound differences between the sexual development of men and women – differences which once viewed were to give rise to extreme feelings of organic envy.

HAVING FUN

Freud would probably have remained a loner had it not been for the publicity given to the United States Declaration of Independence in which the clearly stated words "pursuit of happiness" were promptly interpreted by many to mean free love, and by Freud as wish fulfillment. Acknowledging this pleasure principle, liberated psychologists now called "having fun" a state of "euphoria" – pronounced you-for-her (masculine gender), you-for-him (feminine gender) and you-for-id (Freudian gender), which partly explains why Freud was accused of having a super ego.

SOCIALISTS

Freud described the id as being something that is present from the moment of birth and acts as an invaluable aid in helping to decide what colour clothes should be worn. The id, it was argued, is only concerned with pleasure, nothing else. Being undisciplined, it responds to its own urges. As may be imagined, among the pure traditionalists the rise of the id was viewed with some misgivings and as a result it rapidly got a bad name. The more radical of the socialists, on the other hand, commented that it was a shame that man had something that had to be held down all the time, pumping for an egotesticle approach which allowed for greater freedom of movement. This, they felt, would be far more satisfying.

PASSIONATE URGES

As would have been expected, there were still those experiencing many frustrations – those who had tried various approaches but with little overall success. Freud, after being out in the cold for so long, could not wait to analyze their efforts and so promptly formulated a theory of frigidity. He reasoned that in the vast domains of the male unconscious are to be found thinly disguised urges and passions, while in the female, there are repressed ideas and feelings of vital unseen forces which periodically exercise control over amorous thoughts and attempted deeds of man.

HEADACHE

In typical sexist fashion, Freud likened the female to an iceberg in which the smaller part showing above the bedclothes represented the region of consciousness, a headache, whilst the much larger mass below the blankets represented the region of unrelenting unconsciousness

– frigidity. After carefully considering their positions, Freud further reasoned that any man denied pleasure by sexual gratification would, as in days of yore, and after calling upon his god, resort to a violent exorcise. Such a display Freud described as being a frantic, displaced, barefooted fertility dance performed around the bedroom and under the bed and called a "libido-limbo"; presumably it was thought that the heat generated would melt the "berg".

COLD BOTTOM

All this lying around under beds left Freud with plenty of time to think about his theories. Perhaps it was because he was surrounded by so much frigidity that Freud developed, apart from feelings of envy and deprivation, a cold bottom. Being rather basic he promptly labelled this as his "anal" stage of development.

ANGUISH

It was during a particularly spirited fertility performance that Freud's first and phallic fingers of his left hand were well and truly stamped upon. Pleasure rather than pain seeking being his prime objective, Freud let out a cry of anguish, later to become known as his oral stage, which not only served to prematurely consummate the performance above his head but also in true Pavlovian manner served to act as effective aversion therapy for any repeat performances.

BRUISED APPENDAGE

It was a time of real discovery for Freud. Sitting at the bottom of the stairs after being so forcibly ejected from the erogenous zone, he now understood what was meant by displaced aggression. Genitally manipulating his bruised appendage Freud noted a gradual feeling of pleasure and tension reduction which convinced him that he was to emerge from climax after climax ultimately spent but on top.

IMPORTANT DATES IN THE HISTORY OF SEX

BC

1.5m	An amoeba realizes it is bisexual and splits.
1.4m	Other half of amoeba feels displaced. Suffers castration complex.
7000	Organ envy noted in Eden.
6980	Sex discovered. Eden designated no-go area.
2000	Begat causes population explosion.
1898	Sodomites have bad time in city fire, emigrate to California.
487	Buddha contemplates his navel. Decides to go on diet.
367	Plato starts first boy scout troop.
218	Hannibal experiments with hybridization – crosses an alp with an elephant.
41	Cleopatra shows Antony her etchings.

AD

433	Attila the Hun invents Schnapps and mud wrestling.
1066	William the Conqueror tries to teach the English how to do French sex, but they can't learn it.
1458	Caxton publishes first mail-order rubberwear catalogue.
1492	Columbus introduces sex into America.
1565	Queen Elizabeth bans sex in Britain except with herself.
1566	Sir Walter Raleigh pioneers smoking in bed.
1567	Queen Elizabeth's bed catches fire.
1620	Pilgrim Fathers are persecuted for not being gay enough – emigrate to America to be dull and do sex properly.
1788	All British sex offenders transported to Australia.
1850	Dr Livingstone invents missionary position.
1851	Queen Victoria orders that everyone should do sex properly like Dr Livingstone.
1876	Custer's last stand.
1890	Sigmund Freud invents psychology of sex – nobody can do sex properly any more.
1901	Theodore Roosevelt invents the teddy bear.
1982	*How To Do Sex Properly* is published. Everyone knows how to do sex properly again.

SEX AND YOUR STARS

We are publishing here for the first time a horoscope that is believed to hold all the secrets of the sexual universe. Although its origins are shrouded in mystery it has been conjectured that it provides great power over the opposite sex for those who understand its riddles and complexities. Genghis Khan, Cleopatra, Rasputin and Bo Derek are among those believed to have had access to its secrets.

Extensive research over recent years has discovered early references to it in the tomb Kamen Dur, a Pharaoh of a lesser dynasty of Egypt, who in his wisdom was sealed in his tomb with five hundred Nubian virgins while still alive.

It next appears in an early Saxon poem which until 1978 had been interpreted as a simple tale of the sexual prowess of a great warrior, but a digital comparison of early English grammatical patterns and modern Danish travel brochures has provided new insights into the text.

Secret Sun Signs & the

Aquarius
January 21st – February 19th

Just as a thousand tides ago the magnificent Triktii defeated the Earth Mover Masvie, then it shall be true that when the voyage of mercury meets the waters of the lions, the magnificent one Triktii shall bestow his powers upon all that cry. "Na sia da, Na sia dada" at the fourth passing of the new moon. With these powers you shall bring down the barriers of all whom you desire and thy seed shall be scattered far and wide.

Pisces
February 20th – March 20th

The Gods have spoke, the fiery daemons of the heavens have cut across the skys once more. Beware the bearded Sagittarian who is one with the fair Libran, for he has discovered the coupling of souls 'twixt Libran & Piscean. Fear the bearded one for he is mighty and has many brethren.

Aries
March 21st – April 20th

When that Aprill with his shoures soote
The droghte of March hath perced to the roote
Than shall the ram com folland long
To take ewe with his fertil song.

Taurus
April 21st – May 21st

When the moon of the Seven Mountains appears in the west and mars appears in the east, then the great buffalo god shall descend to the forests. His war dance shall echo in the valleys of the Mohawk. Those born in his shadow shall have the fruitful loins of the water squirrel and will be blest with many warriors who shall bring many wives to their father and many beaver skins also, bringing great wealth & respectability to the great white tepee on the banks of the Potomac.

Gemini
May 22nd – June 21st

May 11. I saw a dead hedge-hog curled up by the side of the road. The dandelions were a beautiful sight along the railway embankment. Weather still cold and showery with bright intervals. My sister brought home some beautiful pink worms that she found in a drain outside Croydon.

Other references to it and extracts from it occur in historical documents previously thought to be quite unrelated to this subject, but those who held its secret were unwilling to reveal the source of their power and much of the content remained concealed in a seemingly innocuous form. The Bayeaux Tapestry, the Sistine Chapel, Chaucer's *Canterbury Tales* and, in more recent times, *The Country Diary of an Edwardian Lady*, are all believed to be disguises for this important text.

The edited form presented here was compiled by an eminent Indian astrologer and publisher, Egdirreh Selrahc, while residing in self-imposed exile in a tower in a remote region of the West. His sources were the earliest available reference for each star sign and the text therefore varies considerably in style and cultural background.

Secrets of the Universe

Cancer
June 21st –
July 23rd

Hark the Wombats staring eyes, the possums pointed nose,
let wallabies sing by the light of the moon,
A crab can bite off your toes

Leo
July 24th –
August 24th

As the mighty stars of the North cleaveth into the wilderness of the heavens, thus shall the chariots of the sun bring much opportunity to the lions of that land. But the chariots shall bring great misfortune, that taketh and assheth the unworthy ones into the pits of hell. And so it shall be said that the lions should stay in the custody of their lairs in the custody of those born in the times of Taurus throughout the hours of the day.

Virgo
August 14th –
September 23rd

As sure as the Goth doth pillage, and the Sabine women be raped
So it shall be ye rest intacta, be ye not so perfectly shaped
Yet grieve not O timid one, Your days are not all sorrow
Forsooth shall come a golden prince, Possibly tomorrow

Libra
September 24th –
October 23rd

I am cold as earth, as old as earth and in the earth am I.
One of six to eight. The hills are not as high, the sea so deep
as a dream. Over the water a destination, under the sky
a culmination, seek not the hare in me.

Scorpio
October 24th –
November 22nd

In this year of ye great winds and the moon's dominance
over ye sun goddess in the sign of Virgo, if thou approachest
such a person thou shalt be truly dominant and worthy of
the sign of the scorpion. Ye moons dominance shall also enjoin
thee to undertake ye great journey and be truly successful in all
that thou has chosen to pursue.

Sagittarius
November 23rd –
December 20th

And when the full moon hath passed over thrice and uranus
approacheth the huntress, the archer will sharpen his weapon
and deck it with the feathers of the great bird.

Capricorn
December 21st –
January 20th

Behold, an he goat came from the west, and he had a notable horn.
And he came to the ram that had two horns and ran into it and
there was no power in the ram to stand before him but he cast
it down to the ground and was victorious.

YOUR QUESTIONS ANSWERED

Fred and Lottie Smørgasbord, the world famous brother-and-sister team of sexologists, have spent most of their lives answering questions from the worried readers of their popular magazine *Oooh!* Here we bring you a selection of the most often asked questions and their expert replies.

Hands Up

What is the normal size of a hand? I have heard the saying "Big hands, big feet" and I have got very big feet, but my hands are extremely small. My sister says her mount is 16 hands – is this big?

I take size 8 in gloves and think that must be less than most people. I am 21.

Yes, size 8 is very small and at 21 they are unlikely to grow any bigger. However, you could try doing these exercises which might increase your size a bit.

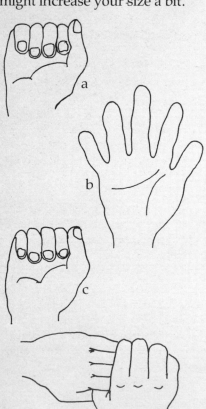

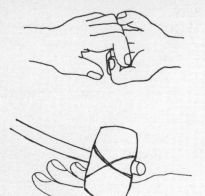

Also, if you wear thick gloves your hand will look bigger.

F. & L. S.

p.s. 16 hands is big for a pony, but quite normal for a horse.

Can *The Borgias* Make Me Pregnant?

Last Tuesday my boyfriend and I were sitting on the sofa watching The Borgias on television when all of a sudden we both fell asleep. I have heard that if you sleep with a boy you can get pregnant and now I am very worried about this. Am I pregnant?

In normal circumstances this is possible, but if, as you say, you were watching *The Borgias* at the time, it is very unlikely.

F. & L. S.

I Want Crimplene

I am a young woman of 25. Ever since I was confirmed I have been very strongly attracted to things made of Crimplene – Crimplene coats, Crimplene dresses, Crimplene trousers and so on.

I wear Crimplene things a lot myself, but it's not quite enough. I have a strong desire to dominate men and this is somehow tied up with my interest in Crimplene.
It has been rather difficult for me to find men to share my interests and lusts in this direction. Can you help me?

p.s. Is there a Latin name for people who like Crimplene?

We have come across this interest in Crimplene only once or twice before, and I am afraid it is very rare in men. You could try advertising your needs in this direction and you may get some replies. But, if this fails, put away your Crimplene for a while and try to form a deep relationship with an ordinary man. If he really loves you he will soon learn to share your interests.

I believe the Latin name for such an interest in Crimplene is *Crimpus limpus.*

Good Luck,

F. & L. S.

Provocative

I am very happy in my job and I am doing very well there. The trouble is my boss. She is always coming up behind me and pinching my bottom and saying lewd things to me.

I can't be rude to her because I am afraid of losing my job. I try to laugh it off and slap her hand and say "Naughty, naughty, Mrs Spieler", but she is becoming more persistent.
Please help me, what shall I do.

It seems to us reading between the lines, that you don't really mind Mrs Spieler's advances. You are no doubt encouraging her by wearing sexy, tight trousers, and bending over when you know she is behind you. There is usually some "contributory negligence" in these cases.

We suggest you wear less provocative clothing – baggy trousers, looser shirts. Leave off the aftershave when at work. Always bend demurely by bending at the knees.

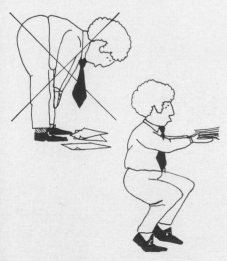

If you find that you are still provoking your boss, perhaps you had better think again about your career. Find a job in an all male environment, that involves less bending.

F. & L. S.

Vile Bodies

I am 21 and have tried to go out with girls several times but I just don't like it. My best friend Kevin feels the same way and we are much happier when we are together than with opposite sex people. We don't think there is anything wrong with the way we feel, do you?

We most certainly do! There is far too much of this sort of thing going on these days. These unnatural practices are striking at the heart of our civilization and we *defy* these evil influences which are seeking to undermine the very foundations of western democracy.

You must both immediately join the armed forces and hope that a bit of martial discipline will knock some sense to you!

F. & L.S.

Filth

My problem is that I think sex in all its form is just filth and it makes me feel sick. I have always been a very clean person, taking three baths a day, changing my clothes each time and my underwear at least six times a day.

I have been married for 14 years and until now have been able to make excuses to my husband but he is beginning to get suspicious. I don't think I will be able to hold out much longer, what shall I do?

You should not worry about these feelings – they are quite normal. Sex is filthy, but we all have to do our bit. We suggest you close your eyes and think of something clean, such as disinfectant.

F. & L.S.

Sex and Your Eyesight

I know that playing with yourself is very bad for you, but I do enjoy it so much. Would it be alright if I did it just until I needed glasses?

The fact that this is alright is proved by the number of people who do have to wear glasses. It is, however, important to have regular check-ups with your oculist who will tell you when to slow up.

F. & L. S.

Heavy Petting

My girl friend and I have been dating for some years now and she says it is time we started to do some "heavy petting".

I am rather worried about this as I am a large football player and Marlene is quite small. I do not want to squash her.

Also I have heard that this can lead to "social diseases".

Should I tell her that I respect her too much to do this, or should I take the risk.

We all have to take risks sometimes. I expect you take risks when you play football, don't you?

If you are frightened of squashing Marlene, you could try the reverse missionary position illustrated on page 24.

The problem of social diseases is more difficult. As you know, germs and microbes are everywhere. You can, however, minimize the risks if you both wear surgical masks when you do heavy petting.

F. & L. S.

GLOSSARY

Abrasion
An injury that can occur when erogenous zones are rubbed too hard.

Afterbirth
A period of sexual inactivity commonly suffered by a husband after the birth of a child. The male equivalent of post-natal depression that can last for the rest of his life.

Anal fixation
A problem that can occur when doing heavy petting in a car with a floor shift.

A car. Note the perilously placed floor shift.

Amoeba
A very advanced animal that has developed a sexual technique that is second to none.

Aphrodisiac
Foods that make you more attractive to the opposite sex such as garlic, snails, frog's legs and horsemeat.

Artificial insemination
Unnatural practices.

Attila the Hun
An expert in "German" sex.

56

Belgians
People who do sex and compulsive stuffing, but not as well as the French.

Bert Weedon
A man with a reputation for great sexual prowess, now used to describe any over-sexed man, as in the phrase "He's a real Bert Weedon".

Bishops
Men who wear frocks. A harmless deviation that is difficult to cure.

Boiled Cod
Take a nice plump cod and put it in a pan of water. Bring to the boil and simmer for one hour.

Borgias, The
A non-habit-forming narcotic – much better than counting sheep.

Breasts
Lumps on the front of ladies, not to be confused with pimples or lumps on the front of men.

Bubonic Plague
A social disease that is very infectious.

Cannibals
People that are taught how to do sex properly by missionaries.

Chiropodist
A person with an unnatural desire to touch other people's feet – see also Ingrown Toenails and Bunions.

Coitus Interruptus
A phenomenon that occurs during sexual relations when a door slams followed by the words, "Darling, I'm home".

Country Diary of an Edwardian Lady
A book of rare genius that holds the secrets of the sexual universe.

Crimplene
A very alluring fabric that drives men wild.

Dribble
An involuntary excretion of saliva that occurs in many ball games.

Egyptian PT
Extremely violent physical exercise that Egyptians dream about during their afternoon naps.

Fact of Life
Anything that can go wrong does go wrong.

French
Pertaining to the people of France who are all superb sexual performers and have lent their name to many sexual terms, hence:

French door – a large window allowing easy egress when caught doing illegal sex – see Coitus Interruptus

French dressing – the ability to dress and undress very quickly

French fry – to dip things in boiling oil – see Deviations

Some sexy Frenchmen preparing for a night of passion.

French kiss – a quick kiss on each cheek given by French people when they want to do sex with you

French horn – a hard pointed outgrowth belonging to a French person

French leave – to leave a social gathering early accompanied by a friend – premature withdrawal

French letter – a very romantic letter as written by French people

French toast – a sexual stimulant – see also Aphrodisiac.

Galtieri, Adolph Idi

A great Latin lover who invented the "Galtieri position", which is too rude to illustrate here but which involves a lot of bondage and domination.

Gigolo

An Irish musical instrument like a small flute.

Heartburn

A peculiar burning sensation felt in the chest when you first see your ideal partner across a crowded room.

Hormones

Little messengers that scuttle around your body and tell it when you are ready to do sex.

Indigestion

Often the result of compulsive stuffing, especially in Belgium.

Jockeys

Small but fast – thoroughly recommended.

Latent sexuality

Sexual relations that take place in a canvas structure set aside for that purpose.

Lone Ranger

Tonto's friend.

Microbes

Tiny invisible insects that float about in the air and are very catching.

Missionary

A person that teaches cannibals and pygmies how to do sex properly.

Stanley met a missionary.

Nymphomaniac

A person with an obsessive desire to assault gnomes and fairies.

Omar Sharif

The thinking woman's Reg Varney.

Orgy

A gathering of like-minded people for discussion of the important issues of the day.

Premenstrual Tension

A form of paranoia experienced by sexual partners following a precautionary lapse.

Protruberance

Any "part" of the body that sticks out, e.g. pimples.

Pygmy

See Missionary.

Reproduction Organs

New organs to replace your old worn out ones that look just like the real thing. It's marvellous what they can do these days.

Rubber

One who rubs.

Rupture

A feeling of intense joy felt by those who are in love.

Sado-necrophiliac Bestiality

Flogging a dead horse.

Sex Drive

An outing in a car that has insufficient fuel.

Socialist

A person that does a lot of socializing – see Orgy and Octopus position.

Social Disease

An infectious illness caused by microbes, very common among socialists.

Sonny Tufts

President of ithe United States.

Tonto

The Lone Ranger's friend.

Vasectomy

The surgical removal of shards of china from a male following a domestic dispute.

INDEX

A

Abrasions 28
Acne 6, *12*, 16
Amoebas 50
Attila the Hun 51

B

Baths, cold 45
Baxter, Warner 16
Bear, Teddy 51
Beastliness 44
Belgians 18, 28, 67, 79, 82, 92, 106 etc
Bert Weedon 52, 56
Bishop, The *24*
Bishops, Some 16
Blonde, A beautiful *11*, 48
Blood, dirty 44
 hot 45
Body, hair 8
 odour 12
Bodies, vile 54
Bondage 27, *42*
Borgias, The 54
Bosoms *11*
Bottoms *11*
 cold 51
Boy Scouts 16, 51
Breasts *11*
Bruises 28
Bunions 44

C

Camels 48
Cannibals 6
Chandler, Jeff 6, 16
Cod, boiled 45
Colonic irrigation 28
Country Diary of an Edwardian Lady, The 52, 53
Crimplene 31, 54, 56
Custer's Last Stand 51

D

Dirt 44
Discipline 29
Disinfectant 55
Dreams, "bad" 45
Dribble 18

E

Earwax *12*
Egyptian PT 29, 56
Elbows 7
Etre, raison d' 50
Euphoria 50
Eyeballs *12*

F

Fascists 6
Filth 7, 44, 55
Fishnet stockings *42*
Flashing *43*
Floppiness 9
French
 door *40*, 56
 dressing 56
 fry 56
 kiss 18, 56
 leave 56
 letter 56
 horn 56
 man *26*, 29
 mistress 28
 people 18, 26
 sex 51
 , The *26*
Freud, Siggy 38, 50
Frustrations 51

G

Galtieri, Adolph Idi (no relation) 56
Garlic 18, 26

Germs 55
Goebbels, Larry 16, *46*
Goering, Harvey 16, *46*
Gratification 51

H

Habits, nasty 44
Hair, body 8
 dry, lifeless, unmanageable 44
 nose *12*
Hairdressers 16
Halitosis *12*, 38
Harvey Goering 16, *46*
Havoc, playing, with 8
Heart attacks 12, 34
 massage 34
Hite, Ms 38
Hitler, Mr A. 16
Hun, Attila the 51

I

Indigestion 45
Ingrown toenails 44
Instinct, deep-rooted 48
It 7

J

Jockeys 28

K

Khan, Genghis 52
Kinsey, Dr Cyril 38
Kleptomaniacs 6
Knees, knock 44
Knock knees 44

L

Larry Goebbels *46*, 47

Last Stand, Custer's 51
Life, The Facts of 46-7
Lone Ranger, The 43
Loud, Ms Gloria 6, 7

M

Microbes 18, 55
Missionary position *24*, 50
    reverse *24*, 55
Muscles, bulging *10*
    flabby 12
    flaccid 12
    glistening *10*
    hard *10*, 12
    rippling *10*
    well-developed *10*, 11
Mud wrestling 16

N

Negligence, contributory 54
Nose hairs 12

O

Oooh! 20, *47*, 54
Orgy 16

P

Pain, excruciating 34
Parkinson, Michael 6
Parts 10
Pervicacious gonadal
    urges 7
Peter Pan 17
Petting, heavy 55
Pictures, lewd 44
Pimples 44
Practices, unhealthy 45
Plastic surgery 18, 35
Possums 52
Protruberances 11, 23
Pustules *12*
Pygmies 6

Q

Quasimodo 16

R

Rowe, Colin – *see* Teddy
    Bears
Rowe, Erica (no relation) – *see*
    Bosoms
Rubber 16, 31, *42*
    far-eastern, imported 42
Ruptures 34

S

Saliva 18
Selrahc, Egdirreh 52
Sharif, Omar 12
Sheep, Australian 27, 31
Sheep's eyes 48
Slobber 18
    excess of 34
Smørgasbord, Fred and Lotte
    54
Snow White 16
Social diseases 55
Socialism 28
Socialists 50
Sodomites 51
Spieler, Mrs 54
Spitting, No, 38
Spittle 18
Somatogenic Stimulative
    Factor 7
Stainless Steel Chain, 30 ft of
    43
Strangulation, danger of 23
Stuffing, compulsive 9
Suicide 27
Superman 17
Sweat, excess of 34

T

Tarzan 16, 29
Tax inspectors 40
Tiitii, the magnificent 52
Tonto 17
Tufts, Sonny 6, 16, 57

U

Urges, pervicacious gonadal
    ones 7

V

Vasocongestive response
    situation 7
Vice, secret 44
Vomit 27

W

Wagga Wagga 7
Water Squirrel, fruitful loins
    of 52
Weedon, Bert 52, 56
Whips 27, *43*
Wombats 52
World Bank, The 7
Worms 16, 53
Wrestling, mud 16

X

Xenophobes 6

Z

Zabriskie's Point 89
Zambians 84
Zealanders 73
Zebras 92
Zephirus 69
Zeppelins 3
Zero 65
Zimbabweans 105
Zippers 22, *23*, 38, 42
Zithers 65
Zombies 67
Zones, erogenous 6, *20*
Zoologist 6
Zoomorphism 72
Zoospore 66
Zorba the Greek 65
Zoroastrianism 69
ZPG 60
Zulus 98
Zwingli, Ulrich 95
Zygotes 6

SO YOU DON'T LIKE SEX

Well, if you've tried all the exercises and have now discovered that sex is just not your cup of tea . . . don't be too disappointed. There are lots of things left to do, such as water-skiing, politics, accountancy, or hanging around public libraries. Of course, you're going to have problems, for there will always be some people who will want to do it with you, and they may not understand when you tell them to stop. So you must be prepared to upset people.

Probably the easiest and least painful way of avoiding these embarrassing meetings is to make yourself unattractive. This isn't as easy as it may sound. Many normal people are attracted to B.O. and halitosis, but if you are persistent and stand on street corners waving empty sherry bottles and swearing at passers-by, you'll keep most away and be able to live out your life of celibacy.

If you're in a well-respected position in employment or in the community, you will have to use a different approach. The best is to master the sly grin, the wink and the throaty chuckle. Practise these in the mirror at home, use them whenever sex comes into the conversation and you will find that your sexually normal associates will never suspect your problem.

Meanwhile, so this book hasn't been a total waste of time, we've included some simple puzzles and games to while away the many hours that you'll have to spare in the evenings.

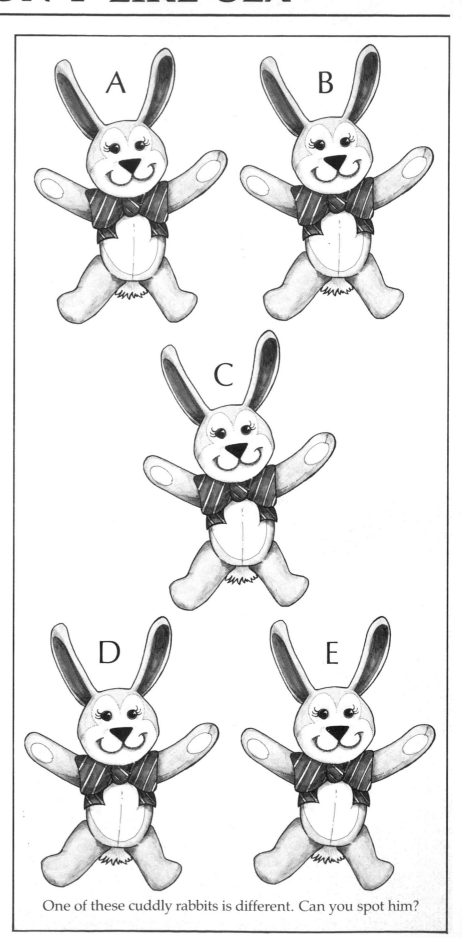

One of these cuddly rabbits is different. Can you spot him?

There are 12 cuddly rabbits hidden in the picture. See if you can find them all. Afterwards you can colour the picture in with your crayons.

MAZE

Find your way down the rabbit warren to visit cuddly granny rabbit.

YOUR DIPLOMA

Now that you have finished this book, you may fill in your name in the space provided on the Certificate of Proficiency. Cut it out and always carry it with you – you never know when you may be asked to produce it.

You may also cut out and wear the badge provided here. Glue it on to cardboard and fix a safety pin to the back with sticky tape.

INTERNATIONAL SEX TRAINING COUNCIL

Certificate of Proficiency

This is to certify that

....

having completed a course of study approved by the Sex Proficiency Board, knows HOW TO DO SEX PROPERLY and may practice sex on consenting adults.

CHIEF TRAINING OFFICER
INTERNATIONAL SEX TRAINING COUNCIL